SETTING OUT FOR THE MAD ISLANDS

SETTING OUT FOR THE MAD ISLANDS

POEMS OF TWO DECADES

ROGER CALDWELL

All rights reserved. No part of this work covered by the copyright herein may be reproduced or used in any means – graphic, electronic, or mechanical, including copying, recording, taping, or information storage and retrieval systems – without written permission of the publisher.

Printed by imprintdigital
Upton Pyne, Exeter
www.imprintdigital.net

Typesetting and cover design by narrator
www.narrator.me.uk
info@narrator.me.uk
033 022 300 39

Published by Shoestring Press
19 Devonshire Avenue, Beeston, Nottingham, NG9 1BS
(0115) 925 1827
www.shoestringpress.co.uk

First published 2016
© Copyright: Roger Caldwell

The moral right of the author has been asserted.

Cover photograph by Matt Benson

ISBN 978-1-910323-42-7

ACKNOWLEDGEMENTS

Acknowledgements are due to the following in which versions of these poems first appeared: *Acumen, Ambit, Great River Review (*US*), Interchange, The Interpreter's House, London Magazine, Orbis, Poetry* (Chicago*), Poetry Scotland, Poetry Wivenhoe, Seam, The Seventh Quarry, Stand.*

'John Steed in Retirement' received first prize at the 2014 Essex Poetry Competition, 'The Tunnel: A Question in Philosophy' was a commendation in the same competition. 'A Defence of Essex' was highly recommended in the 2014 Lumen/Camden Poetry Competition

'Survival of the Fittest' and 'Late Elizabethan' appeared in the pamphlet collection, *Walking on the Moon* (Ninth Arrondissement Press).

"This is poetry, Lucy," said Ravenswood, "and in poetry there is always fallacy, and sometimes fiction."

(Sir Walter Scott, *The Bride of Lammermoor*)

CONTENTS

ONE

The Taste of the Real	3
The Velvet Band: A Tale from the Fin De Siècle	4
Tristan or The Truth of the Text	6
Nietzsche Contra Grammar	8
Little Lord Nobody	9
Pecksniff as Hero	11
Trouble with Workers: A Report from the Director	13

TWO

Early Days: A Scene from the Pre-Cambrian	16
Survival of the Fittest	18
Orichalc	20
Remembering Leontius	22
Pharsalus	23
Dirge for the Old Icelandic Poets	24
The Emperor	26
Late Elizabethan	28
London 1665: A Witness Speaks	29
Drawing the Line	31
Upstream, Downstream: After Jerome K. Jerome	33
Voyage of the Patagonia	34
Virginia Woolf in War-time	36
The Reluctant Colonialist: Graham Greene in Sierra Leone	38
Auden at Kirchstetten	40
Helmand Province	41
Return of the Soldier	43
Breathless in Jerusalem	44
Tiananmen Square: A Lesson in Mathematics	46
Icelandic Saga	47
The Statue in Your Head	49

THREE

The Seventh Room	53
Our Differences	55
Another Sort of Midnight	56
John Steed in Retirement Remembers Mrs Peel	58
The Tunnel: A Question in Philosophy	60
A Defence of Essex against Mere Prejudice	62
The Twilight Zone	64
Hertford Castle	67
As a Man Grows Older	68
Setting Out for the Mad Islands	70
The Picnics	72

Notes 73

One

THE TASTE OF THE REAL

Brought by the courteous yet enigmatic waiter,
it lies before you on the plate
so different from what the menu promised
that at first you think there has been some mistake –
there's something squirming in the sauce,
elsewhere a sort of twisted fin obtrudes.

Your first instinct is to get up and leave –
if this town's cuisine is "anything but bland"
it has brought you more surprises than the guide-book promised.

As the last side-dishes are brought on
(whose appearance fails to reassure)
and the waiter bows out with a mumbled phrase
that might be translated as *bon appétit*
though it as much sounds like a gypsy's curse,
you realise that time is getting late
and accept no better food's on offer.

You must overcome your queasy palate,
put aside your doubts and apprehensions,
take up the waiting knife and fork,
spear up the quivering morsels for yourself,
act nonchalant, begin to eat,

yet knowing as you do so that the taste
of reality – so sharp, so strong, so strange and new
to one who has subsisted on its substitutes –
will linger on your tongue your whole life through.

THE VELVET BAND: A TALE FROM THE FIN DE SIÈCLE

The old count – she has endured his antediluvian pleasantries for the last half hour –

for some reason known only to himself has embarked on a Chinese parable, while across the table

her husband glowers (he is being talked at by a diplomatic guest in all-too-fast and fluent French)

and is tapping, absent-mindedly, with impatient fingers on the tablecloth. The doctor on her right

will only speak in English (or what he considers to be English), even his moustache

is resolutely Anglo-Saxon. To her left the Chinese parable is still drawling on, although by now

more hesitant and fragmentary than before, through intermittent teeth. She's toying with a silver fork,

investigating what look like sea-shells, spearing slices of spiced cucumber, morceaux of seasoned broccoli:

there's little on the dish that looks substantial. Her husband, she's aware, can't keep his eyes

away from her: he knows she's looking at her best tonight and will maybe never look as good again.

He suspects that she's discovered something, whether in a briefcase or a hidden bureau drawer,

it's this that gives her eyes a special look. She's maybe seen the velvet band, and drawn conclusions,

and certainly the way she's dressed is not for his sake, nor the
doctor's, nor the count's. Meanwhile

the Chinese parable, it seems, has drawn to an end at last, though
quite what the point of it was,

no one can tell, his speech was slurred so, and now they're bringing
on another side-dish, it seems to be a sort of seaweed salad,

no wonder everyone demands more claret. Her husband says
"Enchanté" to the diplomatic guest,

then kisses gallantly some lady's outstretched hand, but he sees her
eyes are on the double door behind him

even as she's nodding to the count, and saying sweetly "How
profound", lips pursed a little,

and he wonders now what parable he's in, and in what language the
denouement will occur

as she lays aside her decorated fan, and pushes with her silver fork
from side to side

uneaten salad pieces on her willow-pattern plate.

TRISTAN OR THE TRUTH OF THE TEXT

(1)

No longer sole possessor of her charms –
if that he ever was –
he saw that she spoke truly to the word:

By God I've lain in no man's arms
but yours, and those of that beggar there
who helped me across the muddy ford.

Then, lifted out of his despair,
he declared in truth that she could speak no lies –
but found a coldness meet his warm embrace
which made him doubt once more
who had good cause to then recall
the long look in that beggar's eyes.

(2)

He would have believed it anyway –
then within a moment disbelieved it,

since everything he saw gave sign
that something drastic was amiss:

the likelihood, unlikelihood
of what he'd constantly supposed

or else denied at such high cost
meant nothing but what love he'd known,

whatever truth or lies were now,
was something he'd forever lost.

(3)

The words themselves were true, of course:
he saw by the way she said them
they were true to her,
though spoken to a dunce,

but that she *had* to say them
and as if by rote
meant an end as both knew
to what words were once.

NIETZSCHE CONTRA GRAMMAR

This is a sentimental and deluded race
enamoured of their language-games,
too much seduced by their own words –
they have a desperate faith in grammar,
in a reality that answers to linguistic whims.
They speak, nonchalant, of immortality,
of freedom, justice, and, because the words exist,
think to magic up a world that fits their words,
a universe that honours merely *human* need.

And then they call on God (though God
has left no calling-card to answer)
to grant them worthy of a universal love –
but love's a bitch as much as reason is
that would make of all existence its own mirror,
write out the world in perfect sentences
and with a full stop at its furthest point
so that nothing may perish or dissolve
of all that human beings thought, felt, did –

as if that mattered in the scheme of things,
as if this weren't a world of change
where nothing's set in stone, and even less
the solecisms they inscribe on it:
they are themselves grammatical mistakes.

This is a species to be superseded,
none of their many words can save them.
I make mine plain, as plain as riddles are,
which, once you've solved them, can be put aside,
having seen that words are only – *words*.

If no one understands me now, they will –
too late – and on the other side of language.

LITTLE LORD NOBODY

At parties in Mayfair they chatter and laugh –
for them life is a feasting with no aftermath –

but if they turned to the window they'd see through the rain
Little Lord Nobody's face at the pane,

for he casts on the world an inquisitive eye
which looks out on life as life passes him by.

He would that he too were a person of worth
but the ticket he holds says: *No place on this earth*.

The famous, the rich fall in love at a whim.
As for Little Lord Nobody – no one wants him.

Yet he swears as he passes you by on his way
that he will be powerful too one day

and ride like you in a great limousine
with a hundred photographers on the scene,

and manage astutely matters of state,
and at embassy functions he'll never be late,

but these are things that at present he cannot discuss
as Little Lord Nobody runs for a bus.

If they knew of his presence they'd snigger or sneer
at the Small One, the Humble, who sips at a beer,

who, looking at history's pattern, infers
the great revolution that never occurs

and, denouncing his rulers and their crimes,
dies unmentioned in *The Times*.

But that explosion of envy through the sky
is Little Lord Nobody's soul whizzing by,

so if at a Palace party one day
the rainclouds appear and the sun fades away

and heaven falls open and drenches you through,
know – it's Little Lord Nobody pissing on you.

PECKSNIFF AS HERO

Through dewy ferns from which
a startled hare leaps up,
past mantled pools where busy gnats
whirr round in one
contracting then expanding circle,
well-corseted, the worthy Pecksniff walks.

In hollow places, over fallen leaves,
through meadow-grass, past hedges
fragrant with wild roses,
his pious eyes raised up to heaven,
and in a sort of holy calm,
contemplative, he treads his godly path.

It's as if he has no eyes to fathom out
the fair young form of Martha Graham
on the way ahead, no ear to hear
the enticing rustle of her petticoats,
thus it would be blasphemy to think
he has his hands already round her nubile hips –

so when her scream rings on a sudden out,
and there are running feet, he is perplexed.
He meant no harm, he merely tried
to save her from a fall on muddied ground,
and if the poor girl misinterpreted
his act of providence, then he forgives her.

They may say he is a smooth-tongued lying rogue,
they may accuse him – Pecksniff! – of hypocrisy,
he will not choose to think the less of them,
but merely hopes in time they'll come to see
that God, and truth, are on his side.
He walks on with affronted dignity.

He's imperturbable, the rock of righteousness.
It's as if the poor girl's cry of shock
were an enigma still awaiting resolution,
as if he, Pecksniff, much maligned,
were nonetheless the hero of the tale,
would be revealed as such in Chapter 53.

TROUBLE WITH WORKERS: A REPORT FROM THE DIRECTOR

There have been problems with our labour-force –
some workers, imbued with foreign ideas,
think assembling iPods is beneath them,
and decadent hotheads, shirking their duties,
have chosen to jump from factory windows,
thus meeting their deaths on the paving below.

Such behaviour is selfish, and in disregard
of company policy. It must cease forthwith.
All employees now will be urged to sign contracts
promising not to kill themselves,
and to report on colleagues who appear depressed:
we will then take measures to cheer them up.

In the meantime, for reasons of personnel safety,
I have ordered that nets be fixed to the walls
all around the building, so if any still choose,
against regulations, to leap out of windows
they will be caught in their fall, and thus survive –
after suitable therapy – to resume
their rightful place on the production line.

It may be the case that some of our managers
have been too lax, and lack requisite skills
for training workers to fulfil their tasks
to the optimum level, and for this purpose
I have asked the director of the Taipei Zoo,
much experienced in the ways of animals
and how they may best be contained,
to address our managerial staff,
thereby offering much-needed guidance
on how to deal with our own work-force too.

Two

EARLY DAYS: A SCENE FROM THE PRE-CAMBRIAN

It was another lazy sun-baked afternoon –
no movement on the rocky shore,
no sounds but those made by the waves.

Far out to sea a newly-risen island
belched out a steamy cloud of smoke and fumes;
when the wind turned there was sulphur in the air.

There were blue-green smears spread over rocks,
mats iridescent under sunlight's glare:
This was life, but not life as we know it.

It had been like this two billion years.
There seemed no reason things should change.
When darkness fell the same bright stars shone down.

With morning there came warmth, and piercing light –
jagged rocks and seas were as before.
Nothing scuttled with claws among crevasses,

no fish swam in the water, on dry land
no plants, no trees, or birds to fly among them,
no whirrs of insects – all was silence.

So much might never come – or should.
Yet there were signs: that shiny blue-green slime
had advanced across the rocks an inch or two.

SURVIVAL OF THE FITTEST

They came here out of forest shadows,
stumbled into blinding light,
first of their kind on the wide savannah.

They are clever. They are dangerous.
Have learned already how to live
alongside baboons and sabre-toothed cats.

Now as well they can make fire,
can chisel rock and fashion knives
from basalt that will slice through flesh.

They have no names as yet
for animals and plants, for sun and moon,
haven't learned to bury their dead with flowers.

That will all come later.
It's mid-morning of their strange new world.
The noisy horde are gathered round

a bloodied carcase on the river-bed.
One squats alone on a stony ridge,
surveys the broad terrain below,

looks past wind-stunted pines and copses
to the deep blue arc of sea beyond –
as if he would stare into the future.

Then, bending down to cool his hands,
peers into a pool of still clear water,
for the first time sees the face there as his own.

He has no words to frame the questions
Who am I? and *Must I also die?*
but howls an animal cry of pain,

runs back across the warm volcanic dust
to eat with others of his kind.
Leaves behind impressions of his naked feet.

A thousand thousand generations later
we study the imprint of his toes
who at last know what survival means,

that what's left of us will be what's left of him:
an ape-man palate with one molar tooth,
and a wrist- or talus-bone.

ORICHALC

There was an island once
men called Atlantis, its inhabitants
were blessed with mines of silver, gold
and a metal never seen before (or since)
that gleamed a fiery red:
they named it "orichalc".

With knowledge men have since forgotten
they carved out of cliffs their hollow docks
where triremes moored from all the world about.
The royal city was a wondrous place –
on its roads stomped elephants with catafalques.
Its pavements were all lined with orichalc –
it was as if you walked through fire
(though with no corresponding pain, of course).

A little way outside the city was a sacred spot
where the temple of Poseidon in a shady grove,
half-hidden from the sun, was built.
On a high pillar all the great god's laws
were engraved with letters framed by fire
and formed (as you might guess) of orichalc.
Here, each year, disguised in ragged robes,
in secret, monarchs of Atlantis came
and knelt in piety, swore solemn oaths:
that they'd follow his divine requirements –
which they afterwards (or for the most part) did.

To no avail. Like any other race
that of Atlantis too would disappear one day.
And that day came: one afternoon –
children at their play, full-laden ships
jostling for entrance at the port,
men writing books they thought would last forever –
the earth beneath them quaked, seas rose,
and all the island sank beneath the waves,
its people, pleasures, knowledge gone
to mud, and to the bottom of the ocean.

It was as if Atlantis had been just a dream,
the island, and its treasures, lost.
Gold and silver are about us, precious still,
but not the least trace left in all the world –
or none that anyone can find –
of what they had in plenty in their mines,
once rich with fiery seams of orichalc.

REMEMBERING LEONTIUS

Leontius was a man who liked to look at corpses.
The look, the gaze, was all-sufficient:
he had no need to fondle, to let fingers stray,
relishing the feel of lifeless marbly limbs.
Yet the compulsion in itself was troublesome,
set him apart from other men.

Athens was too full for him
of handsome healthy sunburnt faces,
so when he saw a young man with a chalky pallor
he stood entranced, looked on, admired –
could only think how good a corpse he'd make.

Leontius loved life, was not in thrall to death,
adored his wife, and doted on his children,
yet one night he crept into the mortuary,
saw by his lantern on cold slabs
perfection in the bodies lying there,
their breathless breasts, serene and still,
their souls flown off to Hades' kingdom.
He could have stood there for a cold eternity.

It was only self-respect, a sense of duty,
made him turn away, and slink back home
through silent moonlit city streets
to what he should have treasured most
were he the man he'd always hoped to be.

But in Athens there could be no secrets –
there was always someone who would spy them out –
and for all his genial humours, good deeds done,
what he had of virtue was forgotten.

         To posterity
he'd be of no account except that he,
Leontius, was the man who liked to look at corpses.

PHARSALUS

Caesar, after battle, came to Pompey's tents,
saw them wreathed with myrtle-boughs.
Inside were dining-tables dressed with flowers,
and drinking-vessels, bowls of wine
set out ready for the victory-feast
that Pompey, vain, presumptuous,
an old man past his best,
had taken for his due at Pharsalus.

He all but pitied him, his enemy,
though once his friend, who'd fled –
Pompey "the great", his greatness gone,
now with few supporters, in uncertain exile.

On the battlefield at Pharsalus
Romans lay slaughtered by their fellow-Romans.
If he, Caesar, had the victory
the triumph had come dear enough.
He too was past the prime of life,
was bald, and prone to epileptic fits,
but he would indeed be master over Rome –
in the four brief years still left to him.

DIRGE FOR THE OLD ICELANDIC POETS

Otto the Black, and Thorleik the Fair,
and Bragi the Old,
Thorolf, and Thorvald,
Thorkel Hamarskald –
so many poets
skilled at kennings,
writing ornate verses,
praising dubious deeds, obscure virtues
of Norwegian kings
or earls of Orkney
in those distant, desperate,
and bloodthirsty times –

so many battles won or lost,
limbs severed with an axe-swing,
heads shorn off,
so many glaives and gavelocks,
swords night-bringers
to ale-sated courts.
What is it in this mayhem that deserves
such exquisite metrics
and word-cunning?

Sure, there's still that ever-rocking
and man-swallowing
whale-road,
but all hawk-spirited lords are gone,
praise-poets too –

Valgard, Orm, and Einar,
Hallvard, Hallfrod,
Grani, Arnor, Kolli Prudi
all recited *drápas*
and met due applause
(or raucous laughter)
when the mead of poetry was everywhere,
though now it's it all drunk up.

Thor's gone away to eastern parts,
no doubt he's busy killing trolls.
No one goes as guest to Asgard
or seeks wisdom from the norns –
what wisdom did they ever have? –
and even the world-ash itself
is turned to ashes.

Now through winter nights
snow falls as heavily as ever,
as it did a thousand years ago,
obliterating tracks once left
by Eilif's feet
departing from the mead-hall
when carousing ceased,
and those of Steinthor,
Egil Skallagrimson,
Ulf, and Eyvind,
Reg, and Glum.

THE EMPEROR

> "I know I am dead and damned: I am a man possessed by the devil"
> (Rudolf II, 1576-1612)

There is something wrong. He will not see
his confessor, Johann Pistorius of Nidda.
Don Guillén de San Clemente clicks
his Spanish ambassadorial heels in vain.
Saint Lawrence of Brindisi with his retinue
of Capuchin monks is bristling with holy
indignation. High on the hill against the city
he has immured himself within the Hradchin walls,
receives practitioners of the occult, and Jews,
and other heretics, forgets affairs of state.
Where are the Pernsteins, Vratislav the Chancellor,
the lords of Hradec, and the Dietrichsteins
from South Moravia? The Bishop of Olomouc?
The evil Wolfgang Rumpf, High Steward,
President of the Council, much in league with Spain,
keeps quiet his scaly tongue. The Emperor holds court
with Ogier Ghislach de Busbecq who has brought
the tulip from the east, neglects to ratify
Carillo's treaty with the Prince of Transylvania,
has séances instead with Doctor Dee, discusses
Simon Simonius of Lucca's works (bitterly attacked
for his apostasies by Squacialuppi in a pamphlet
that latterly appeared in Kraków). The invenzioni
of the goldsmith Hans Vermeyen take his fancy,
Erasmus Habermel's automata and artificial fountains.
Outside there's talk of war. Here Theobald Hock
presents his book of verses *Schönes Blumenfeld*
which (so he says) suggests a true philosophy of nature
while Judah Loew ben Bezalel, the "celebrated" rabbi,
raises up the golem, and the learned Doctor Kroll opines
that the decomposition of a basilisk
produces scorpions. Here all is devils, demons,
and an emperor possessed. Such vanities – what good

will come of them? For this the ancient Wenceslas Crown,
the Order of the Golden Fleece? Mardochaeus de Nelle
peddling Paracelsan remedies, the Gemma Augustea
purloined from Paris, the alchemical mass (accursed)
of Nicholaus Melchior of Szeben, an unholy host
of cabbalists, hermeticists, magicians? And not least
the crazed Johannes Kepler contemplating stars?

LATE ELIZABETHAN

All ruffs, and furs, and farthingdales,
shrouded cadavers on marble tombs,

tall windows with mullions and transoms,
emblazonings of bogus coats of arms –

here I live by candlelight, won't hear the cries
of fishwives, orangewomen, chimney-sweeps.

The street outside's too narrow to receive
coaches or carts. No costermongers call.

My windows are all shut and caulked,
doors padded with flock-bed or with quilt.

Very fine garters I can do without.
I have not dined on pheasants, godwits, lampreys.

I am not of the Queen's Men, or Lord Chamberlain's.
My name is not Orlando Gibbons

but I have heard lute, cithern, and bandora play.
I have seen the pillared porticoes and fluted pilasters.

I have visited the Long Gallery.
In my metopes place what ornaments you may,

for I am already my sarcophagus.
Am obelisk, cartouche, and scrapwork scroll.

LONDON 1665: A WITNESS SPEAKS

"death now began not, as we may say, to hover over every one's head only,
but to look into their houses and chambers and stare in their faces."
(Daniel Defoe, *A Journal of the Plague Year*)

Bills of mortality were such in Cripplegate,
in Clerkenwell, to keep the sickness out
men closed shutters up, and locked their doors,
and cowered within, though soon enough
it would place its mark on most of them,
having seeped through walls, infected every room.

Those who could departed for the countryside,
wagons laden with their household treasures –
and all too often carried plague along with them.
Soon London's streets were desolate by sunset,
since few dared venture out into the night,
and then few chose to venture out by day.

Hired watchmen guarded houses, death-carts came
at dusk to gather up the buboed bodies,
to be descanted, pell-mell, into pits dug deep
to receive lost souls, all lacking obsequies.
Even proud ones, cynics, bent their heads and prayed
that all would soon be over. This was not to be.

At last so many perished that men's hearts were hardened –
they only looked to shift out for themselves
as sickness crossed the river, came to Southwark,
and in those maddened and distempered times
they grew credulous of prophecies and old wives' tales,
so necromancers prospered in their cheating trade.

More voices were then heard than ever spoke
and apparitions were observed in empty skies,
an angel in St Giles's – so men claimed,
but I was there, I looked, saw no such marvel –
yet for all the fortune-tellers, and quack-conjurors
with charms, and mountebanks with potions

all the more red crosses marked infected houses.
Few services were held, instead vacated churches
told us ministers of God were struck down too.
So prodigal the pestilence became among us
the dead threatened to outnumber those still living,
as if all of London were to be a single silent tomb.

Then winter came at last, sharp sudden frosts
and cold clear air, and by some miracle
even those whose bodies bore the dreaded signs,
though suffering much pain, went on to live,
to be made sound again – the curse was lifted.
As for myself, I thank you, God, that I was saved,

that I can stand on London Bridge, admire the view,
see boats for hire, see ships docked at the wharves –
things I never hoped to see again in those dark days –
though I don't deign to ask of Providence why I survived
to be a witness, or why God's plan required
such suffering, so many dead, that year.

DRAWING THE LINE

I too was an habituée – we thought it chic –
at Madame Strindberg's place, The Golden Calf,
off Regent Street, where in those days
the long-haired literati came –

Ezra – he was there that night,
bearded, histrionic, with a turquoise ear-ring,
acting poet to excess – and Katherine –
Katherine Mansfield, that is, in a Chinese robe –
chinoiserie was then in fashion.

It was the year before the Russians came,
the *ballets russes*, I mean – Nijinsky's leap
in *Le Spectre de la Rose* –
we saw it as the leap into a future
that might yet be ours. But yes, my dear –
the war, of course, put paid to that.

Yet nonetheless there'd been a change –
I'm speaking of a day in Nineteen Ten
and Madame Strindberg's chalk-white face –
her stern demeanour, strident voice
commandeered expressionist theatricals –
they were mercifully brief that night –
and then a rather ragged band struck up
so that daring couples took the floor,
danced the turkey trot, the bunny hop.

Don't ask me why – I'm getting to the point –
so much has intervened since then
when we all saw Madame Strindberg roused
in Swedish indignation, and she said of someone –
I never could quite find out who –
in her strange and heavily-accentuated English,
and loud enough that everyone could hear:

"Yes, I'll *sleep* with him, but *talk* with him,
why, that's something I could never do.
Somewhere one must draw the line."

UPSTREAM, DOWNSTREAM: AFTER JEROME K. JEROME

Days on the river: upstart clerks
with handlebar moustaches, wearing
stripy blazers, and young socialists
in knickerbockers, earnest girls
reading classics in new Everyman editions.

Innocent times – those small secure Arcadias,
when playing the banjo was all the rage,
young couples spooning in the summerhouse,
and three spruce wasters out on a spree,
snaking their way upriver to Shepperton.

But no, not even the dog was innocent,
the summer merely one of many. Mackintoshes,
unfurled umbrellas against driving rain
can't shroud what's floating on the river,
hair outspread, the dead face calm.

Even after this the games will go on,
if at first subdued, for fun's to be had
under the willows at Kempton Park
at five o'clock. New patterns on the water
as a boat turns this way, and then that.

Stories from long ago, of course,
and fashions change, but even now you'll find
someone rowing hard to Maidenhead
against the current – and an upturned boat
that's floating, slow, downstream.

VOYAGE OF *THE PATAGONIA*

> "I thought you thought that everything signified. You were so full," she said, "of signification."
> "Yes, but we're further out now, and somehow in mid-ocean, everything becomes relative."
> (Henry James, *The Patagonia*)

(1)

Gone the closed movie theatres, dogs
loping down deserted streets, gone whitewashed quays
    and Happy Eaters of America –
now the grey dangerous sea spreads far around,
isolating the great ship from something
    greater still. Mere passengers, we're not
the men and women we once were, we own
no country now, and in a gap of time breathe free
    a stateless air, for all
that we're imprisoned on a floating island,
inhaling sea-tang while our deckchairs slant
    at a new angle to normality.

(2)

I pace the deck, am Henry James adjusting
rhythms of a somewhat convoluted prose
    to the lull and swell
of a sullen ocean, working with a subtle mind
though on unwelcome subjects. See him strut,
    that handsome vain young gentleman,
and smoke an extinct brand of cigarette. I write
in faultless copperplate on yellowed page
    Voyage of the Patagonia. I decree
this ship in Liverpool will deck a body
emptier than it set out, and that a fool will find
    no grateful bride to step ashore.

Waves break against the hull meanwhile.
I estimate: this one will, given latitude, achieve
    the farther shore of time,
wherever time may be; this will die mid-ocean;
and this, while I adjust my necktie, serve
    to recompense the voyage out.

(3)

No longer Henry James, or fiction, disembarked
from the tail-end of another era, to a Mersey
    denuded now of shipyards, river
of old hulks and dreams, I stroll, portentous still,
my sentences inconsequent behind me, down
    deserted wharves where new dogs howl,
where relatives turn absolute, all signifies
an age, a time, an island-home, not saying more
    than what's contained inside parentheses.

VIRGINIA WOOLF IN WAR-TIME

Writing isn't an easy task.
not like feeding the goldfish, or playing bowls,
or going to one of Angelica's concerts
on a fine soft summer Saturday evening
and not needing to listen –

although to what effect does a phrase,
and then a sentence, form
and curve under one's fingers
when the mind is as tight as a ball of string,
a sentence somehow binding together

a meeting with Morgan at the London Library
with a million or more of men at arms,
with all the flutterings, flounces, and flings
of a charwoman's duster,
with the hands of a clock at five past three
holding fast to a Wednesday afternoon
as I light the last cheroot in Sussex?

Now life is manoeuvres yet again
and England is all roast beef and beer
as shadows of giant aeroplanes
perplex the Downs, and bombs have fallen
on ceilings, on china in Mecklenbergh Square,
and the room is rubble where I wrote my books.

We live on haddock, hope and sausage-meat.
I shall order macaroni from what's left
of London – I shan't go hunting shoes again
at a Fortnum's sale, or stroll down Regent Street,
won't be searching for whitebait in Selfridges,

since even simply shelling peas
now seems like a sort of sacrament,
as in the Sussex countryside
I meet war, and literature, and middle age,
and know that, if writing's a difficult art,
then so is that of living, loving, dying.

We've no children to survive us, Leonard,
merely books – and now that we have come to live
with our noses pressed to a closed door
I can only ask you to preserve my books.

Preserve them well.
They were both life and death to me.

THE RELUCTANT COLONIALIST: GRAHAM GREENE IN SIERRA LEONE

Here I lie late in the mornings, if I can,
    and feel that time is somehow running short.
Last night's rains began with sudden squalls
    and thunder, and then fell pell-mell,
turned all the ground to swamp, and when they ceased
    an endless whirr of horse-flies came,
made sleep impossible. The lamp's pale glow
    showed rats were swinging from the curtains.
Outside starved pye-dogs started up their howl
    as if at some new-discovered moon.
I dozed from time to time, and had bad dreams –
    I was back in England at some point,
in Trafalgar Square with crocodiles and drums,
    then woke, unrested, to a strangely silent dawn
of puddles, mud, a vulture perching on the iron roof
    as if to tell me something. But it's strange,
I've lost so many of the fears I had back home,
    of spiders, snakes, much other childish stuff
it shames me to remember now, in Africa.
    I've learned to take each day that comes
for what it's worth, not fuss about tomorrow –
    that's what the natives do, and they should know.
You can't make of Africa another England.
    I do what I am paid for, at the office
(if you can call it such) respond to messages
    from London, few of which deserve replies –
like the mosquitoes they arrive in hordes.
    Does anyone in Carlton Place know what it is
that we are doing here, whose purposes we serve?
    Have any of them looked into a native's eyes,
to see them flinch, then turn away, as I do daily?

    Only in laughter, and in acts of love,
does England meet with Africa – though not for long, I think.
    Nor can I say I love my fellow-countrymen as much
as one might hope, but in the evenings, once my maid
    has ironed for me a fresh white shirt,
I bring out my old school tie, am off to the Colonial Club,
    there to greet the washed-up madam at the bar.

AUDEN AT KIRCHSTETTEN

What kind of marriage is it
when one partner only wears a ring
and the other needs to be kept on a chain?

He thought he'd sailed into a sea of calm,
that all the demon dogs had been released.
There was a certain naïveté in this:

after so much searching for the Great Good Place
was perfection then a map of body-parts?
Between Kierkegaard and Marx

he seeks a safe enchanted fairy-spot,
Kirchstetten, say, with crossword-puzzles,
recalling that spoiled angel's lost good looks.

HELMAND PROVINCE

The first syllable is right
though it should be written with a double 'L':

barbed wire, desert, forty in the shade,
and mines left by the Soviets, and IEDs*

laid with exquisite malice by the Taliban
down all-but-trackless sand-swept roads,

so when human eyes, minesweepers, fail,
as they are apt to do, a blast might mean

at best another soldier maimed, at worst
more routine condolences sent home.

Helmand Province is a place for connoisseurs,
no nursery for neophytes, of war –

from wadis, or from poppy fields,
or what's left of small neglected townships

where smiling children play and the single shop
sells only motorcycle parts and Calorgas,

the roar of an engine revving up
might mean another spy is setting out,

though as it fades through dust-filled air
there comes a frightened silence part-redeemed

by a holy man who chants the call to prayer,
a jackal's bray from way out in the wilderness.

---

* IED: acronym for Improvised Exploding Device

And then close gunfire, cordite, smoke,
a bomb or a grenade gone off, and running feet,

and panic, though through suffocating heat
come the crackling of a radio and, with luck,

the reassuring sound of Chopper blades,
an Apache circling overhead, and hope.

I too once ventured to Afghanistan.
found peace in Herat, and smoked Afghan gold,

was young (as they are), never ventured far,
not to Kabul, Kandahar – or Helmand Province

where, it's said, the stars by night shine down
more bright than any other place on earth,

though no one with a choice would choose
to venture out to marvel at them now.

RETURN OF THE SOLDIER

I wasn't any more the son you knew
when I came back. Maybe I looked the same,
or almost so, my body more or less intact
but for some bits of shrapnel buried deep –

yet you must have seen I couldn't meet your eyes,
sensed there were things I couldn't say,
and when I cried out from bad dreams
it must have sounded well beyond the bedroom door.

I couldn't act the same with friends I'd known
before I went out to Afghanistan.
It too much felt that they could read my thoughts.
They could scarcely guess what I'd been a party to
but the way they looked at me put paid
to any ties there'd been between us once.

Ma, Pa, you would have come to hate me too
if you knew all that happened there.
I did what they demanded, maybe more,
then they pumped me full of drugs and sent me home –
once all that I'd believed in had been bombed to bits.

When I returned I was no child of yours –
he'd died out in the desert, or he should have done,
at one with all the others who could not come back,
and nothing of the boy you raised remained
except in fragments
                      So there was no choice,
no enemy was left to me except myself.
That's why I sit out in the car, turn on the radio,
and put a bullet through my head.

BREATHLESS IN JERUSALEM

Here in the Municipal Garden –
all white paths and straggly flowers –

asphalt's hot beneath one's feet,
baked in the harsh sun of Jerusalem.

Tombstones in the Muslim graveyard
among unruly tangled olive-trees

stand secretive – but even here
there's little shade: they are hot to the touch.

Houses, shuttered against noonday heat,
give no hint of what goes on inside.

In narrow alleys of the shopping quarter
what dry flow comes of desert wind

is all-but-imperceptible.
A young soldier on guard at the corner

sweats visibly, has anxious eyes.
Maybe up in orange-grove country,

in bluish hills of Edom far above,
there is a breath of air. But here is none.

From some far distant vantage-point
a watcher with binoculars surveys

the southern suburbs, although what he sees –
if he isn't blinded by the sun –

is a sort of stillness that's infused
with a sense of something yet to come.

All Jerusalem lies swathed meanwhile
in the unforgiving haze of early afternoon.

TIANANMEN SQUARE: A LESSON IN MATHEMATICS

Students rushed to Tiananmen Square,
erected a Statue of Liberty there
so that the people of Beijing
might hear the bird of freedom sing.

They had forgotten Deng Xiaoping
who, raising from an invalid's bed
his eighty-four-year-old wise head,
smiled a patronizing smile and said:

"The Great Liberator once made room
to let a thousand flowers bloom
but once they'd raised their heads made sure
they'd never lift them any more.
These students for all their education
have yet to learn enumeration.
For though a million hold their view
in all of China that's but few.
Dispose of the million who resist –
in all of China they will not be missed –
and a billion heads will then stay cool,
learning better to respect our rule."

The sun shines bright on Tiananmen Square,
gleams on well-scrubbed paving there,
so clean that you would never know
how much blood there needs to flow
for freedom to take root and grow.

The Liberation Army's task, instead,
to find a bullet for each student head,
was to teach all those who would be critics
first to master mathematics.

ICELANDIC SAGA

Sure, there are fishing-boats at anchor
   as before, bleak rugged lava-fields
      stretched out past Keflavík
         look much the same as in the days

when this remote volcanic outcrop
   of the North Atlantic, rich in fish and trolls,
      in geysers, geothermal energy,
         this icy fiery fabled saga-land, became

the world's epitome of cool: Björk
   and Sigur Rós made Northern Lights
      iridescent in the skies of warmer zones,
         all who could afford it made for Rejkjavík

to sip exquisitely at lava-flavoured vodkas,
   prance *à la mode* down Laugavegur,
      be eco-friendly in the Blue Lagoon.
         But sulphur-fumes were in the air,

and David Oddsson, playing Margaret Thatcher,
   lit the match – controls on credit were relaxed,
      rich fish-quota kings and queens reclined
         on leopardskin sofas, told the time

by their Armani watches. More sweetheart deals
   were made with politicians, then a thrusting brood
      of get-rich-quick kids in designer jeans,
         hair slicked back, employed hot money,

dumped junk bonds and toxic assets, left
   indignant losers shredding kroná-notes
      as their private jets flew out on one-way journeys.
         Fat jeeps remained unclaimed in parking lots

when the Landsbanki crashed and meltdown came
    with busted empires, emptied cash-machines,
        and there was no one left to pay the bill
            for Danish truffles at the Hotel Nordicá

or for exotic cocktails at Bar 101.
    There were fewer diners at the Gullfoss Lounge,
        more nervous lookers-on than buyers
            at the Klinglan mall – and yet it seems,

as prayers rise from the Hallgrímskirkja,
    nothimg will douse Mount Hekla's fires
        or move the Vatnajökull glacier by an inch –
            or bring the saga prematurely to an end.

THE STATUE IN YOUR HEAD

There are cheering crowds, of course,
and hearts are lightened
as the statue
begins to totter on its plinth,
as it trembles on the brink of falling,
then is toppled, on a sudden falls,
as it smashes on the pavement,
broken in a thousand pieces.

It is as if
informers, secret policeman,
torturers and executioners
are likewise this day dead,
consigned
(just as their victims were)
to another page of history –

but, then, it's history
that is imbedded deep,
so deep inside a people's brains
it still decides the way they walk,
the way they think,
their every gesture.

So the question that remains is how,
for all the pieces lying there,
for all the broken effigies,
they next may tear the statues down
that are still standing in their heads.

Three

THE SEVENTH ROOM

There are days you wouldn't willingly
leave home – if you can't say exactly why
yet there is something in the air
that seems to mean no good to you:
a false rumour on the breeze, a word, a phrase
let fall from someone's careless mouth
that's on a sudden closed again.

Even here at home there are unfriendly signs,
a rucked-up carpet, torn-up note,
an ornament gone missing from the shelf,
or a footprint in the hall that's not your own.
It's no wonder that you slip away
into the seventh room, and lock the door.

Here you are safe, no whispers follow,
there's no rack on which you might be stretched,
no noose to put your head into.
Nothing much can touch you in the seventh room.

Yet you can't stay hidden there forever.
No hubbub reaches to the seventh room –
it's only in your head that there are breaking sounds
from bulls in china shops, but that's enough
to make you querulous, dissatisfied.

No doubt it's cold out there, it's maybe bitter cold,
and shelter scanty, and friends hard to find,
but it's time to exit from behind closed doors,
unobtrusively to cross the stone parterre,
to meet the world, and open skies, again.

You may still hanker for the seventh room –
sun's bright but there are piercing winds,
and clouds fly over. Nonetheless,
for all the dogs' dinners you expect,
for all your premonitions and your doubts,
this is another day in which
the needle in the haystack might be found,
hell freeze over, and the cows come home.

OUR DIFFERENCES

Your mind, like mine, is its own place.
I cannot peer inside your head.
Things, no doubt, are different in there

to what's in mine, and could we but compare
it may be I see green where you see red,
I soothed, you angered, by a leaf, by grass,

that where you see Stop signs I see: Go ahead,
that my every new beginning is your *coup de grâce*.
We walk the same streets, though at a different pace,

yet we flinch away, as with a stranger's face,
and turn aside to let the other pass.
We each find different meanings in the words we've said –

we're actors on a stage from which all others fled,
but this is neither tragedy nor – quite - a farce.
You and I have many aliases to declare,

and many secrets too we've failed to share.
We cannot share them when we both are dead.
Here it's time that's precious and not empty space –

of which there is sufficient for the two of us,
and all that's passed between us, to be put to bed,
a bed that's made to lie on. So please join me there.

ANOTHER SORT OF MIDNIGHT

You don't much care to answer questions,
do you, Mr C-? Instead you prefer
living on Dream Street, for there
no one invades your personal space
or talks about things that really matter,

and there are times I can only think
you must have done something bad, bad, bad
when you were young, and ever after
sucked on sweets, since otherwise
the taste of a substance sour and strong
would always fester on your tongue.

You live by the mercy of your misconceptions,
turn your back on any audience,
stare out to sea, B-movie style, and, sure,
that is a style of life – we all of us need
our own little piece of the universe,
whatever shape it comes in,

and yet you, Mr C-,
cultivate so secret a persona, and would flee
dogs and interviews as if they were death,
but it's often the case that our lives take turns
that no one (least of all ourselves)
could ever have predicted.

Yours, Mr C-, is no exception,
you're captain of a ship you can't control
though still reluctant to believe so:
                              that is why
this Christmas you're at home alone,
watching the squirrels run along the fence,
while the sky's a sort of iron-grey,
and somehow it will always be like this,
another sort of midnight,
though it's a quarter to three in the afternoon.

JOHN STEED IN RETIREMENT REMEMBERS MRS PEEL

It's that time of year when I must don my mantle of mirth,
take up my cap and bells, Mrs Peel,
and play the fool before my memories: how long ago it seems
since we went out together on our missions.
I remember that curious crease of leather,
and the graceful sinuous way that you moved, Mrs Peel.
Sadly I have grown portly of late, drink too much
in the afternoon, find M.O.D. pensions don't stretch far,
and the Bentley is gone, was sold for scrap
after I inadvertently turned left not right
that fateful day in Milton Keynes.

True, I was a little the worse for wear,
but was thinking of you again, Mrs Peel,
and how on those long-ago missions from Mother,
when you were tied up (and you often were),
I would come with a smile, an umbrella, and a pun
to release you.

              If we had more style than substance
I at least have neither now, live in a world grown sour,
without panache, where nothing's black or white that is not grey,
in which everything tastes too much of Essex
where I now unhappily reside.

I should have asked you when I had the chance
– I often wondered – what became of *Mister* Peel,
if ever there was such a fortunate man,
and I can scarcely do so now, for I confess
I'm no longer the John Steed you remember,
but one awash with wine and pleas and hesitations.

Yet whenever Christmas or cold weather comes
I find Santa Claus brings me remembrances of you
and I see you as the Ice Queen that you were of old.
And now the years have turned us to antiques
may I be at last allowed to call you *Emma*?
And can you bring yourself to call me simply – *John*?

THE TUNNEL: A QUESTION IN PHILOSOPHY

This summer it's been hot, and togas are in vogue,
so too is metaphysics – teenage girls
stand in huddles on the streets dissecting Plato's Forms.
Hoodies also, asking where is truth, what's happiness,
immerse themselves in Aristotle's *Ethics*.
Our postman, once reliable, is now obsessed
with Zeno's paradoxes, zero, and infinity,
and can't see how to get from One to Two.

All of this seems little to the point. I've heard
too many specious arguments, and now I sit
and swelter on the Central Line, to find the train
has slurred to a stop between two stations –
we're deep in a tunnel, and the lights go out.
I hear, as sweat drips down my face,
voices all around me still descanting on philosophy.

"Is life necessary – or contingent? And what use
is a human being?" are the questions asked
by a suicidal gynaecologist.

                                "But it may be
that truth is relative, and numbers only fictions,"
suggests the banker. "What would happen
if the number five were to be abolished?
Could we still count our bonuses in millions?"

"And where", a desperate sea-captain begs,
"is the Archimedes Point, the Plimsoll Line
of certainty, or do sophistries and delusions
protect us from the truth like fragile parasols?"

Then a hapless deconstructionist declares:
"There's no such thing as an objective truth
beyond the tropes of language. We survive
by means of metaphors, must therefore find
another better way of speaking of reality."

But we're stuck in a tunnel, I can only think,
and, whatever a man or a woman is worth,
the hope to survive is real enough,
and the tunnel in which we find ourselves
is no mere concept of the human brain –
though we all of us ask what a tunnel must mean
for those who might never come out of one.

A DEFENCE OF ESSEX AGAINST MERE PREJUDICE

It is not the case that Essex men
have shaven heads, and numerous tattoos,
that they scowl a lot, have prominent stomachs,
nor is it true that they are semi-literate.
On the contrary.
                  It is also slanderous to say
they are products of a barbarous macho culture,
much fuelled by alcohol and ignorance,
malevolence, and sheer stupidity.
In fact young Essex men are renowned
for their love of butterflies and wild flowers,
for liking Latin puns, for their exceptional grace
in flamenco dancing.
                  As for Essex girls
they likewise are more maligned than praised:
the expressions "mutton dressed as lamb"
or "thick as two short planks" are inappropriate.
Essex girls are fastidious and not "tarted up",
but tend toward the intellectual, often to excess.
Their penchant for metaphysics is well-known
as is their love of the Shostakovich string quartets.
They rarely go "out on the razzle", most of them
are teetotal, virginal, and only rarely snort cocaine.
Teenage pregnancies are unknown in Essex.

It can only be a matter of prejudice
that such terms as "Flash Harry" or "Barbie Doll"
are applied to the reserved, rather reticent,
gentle folk of Essex, as elegant in speech
as they are comely of body, people to whom
terms such as "lager lout" or "hot totty"
are enigmas in this place of peace and beauty.

I regard it a privilege to live in Essex.
If you are seeking the brash, the loud, the vulgar
– and village idiots – you should go to Norfolk.

THE TWILIGHT ZONE

Here life is long, but memories are brief:
    there are doors that no one came through,
        stairways leading neither up nor down,
            and walls built up so high

you'll never see what's on the other side of them.
    This is not chaos quite, but it falls short
        of an acceptable distorder. It is called:
            The Twilight Zone. Here home

is never quite where home should be,
    but on another street where everyone
        speaks a language you can't understand,
            and as you fumble with a key

to the house you think your own, some passer-by
    looks on and smiles derisively as if to say:
        You are mistaken. Better go away.
        For no one lives here any more.

This is the Twilight Zone – you're in disguise
    although you never knew it, spend your time
        having sex by mistake with perfect strangers,
            or by numbers, and on unsprung beds,

always waking to a migraine and a sense of something lost.
    That's how it is now, always will be,
        and the last book you'll read from cover to cover
            lies already open at page ninety-three.

Here you need a birth-certificate to show
    not who you are but who you were, and as a proof
        that you were ever born, albeit on a day
            that's scratched out from the almanac.

Your name has been replaced by that of someone else
    you half recall from some sad hallowe'en
        decades ago – a stranger signs your autograph:
            the hand's ornate, but there are letters missing.

When you open up what looks to be a birthday card
    you find a bill of lading there instead –
        someone should have said you're way off limits
            though there's no one left to tell you so

who's not himself gone way off limits too,
    not also crossed a bridge too far – unless
        it wasn't far enough in such a place as this
            where bridges are erected only to be burned.

Sure, there'll be boats waiting at the creaking quay –
    you can climb aboard, you need no ticket,
        but they'll not set out, not if you pry too much
            about their purpose or their destination.

Day-trips hereabouts might well take weeks, and some
    boats have left the harbour and not yet returned.
        If most – for safety's sake – have never left their moorings
            it's not the nervous passengers who are to blame

but the disgruntled and already seasick sailors.
    Back in town the pavements are another shade of grey
        than any you are used to – you've become
            more careful where you walk, and rightly so:

there are obstacles, holes open up beneath your feet.
    Here you must be more frugal of your hopes,
        less desolated by your disappointments, so
            you're freer of illusions than you were.

But maybe that's illusion too, and you've become
    too much a walking paradox, enigma to yourself
        as you have been to others. For this is a place
            you never thought that you would ever enter

and now find it is a place you cannot leave.
    Every step you take is in another country now
        than any you have known before. You're not alone in this:
            down hill- and mountain-sides, across the plateaux,

or along half-hidden paths, not knowing quite
    what they are doing – as for the most of them,
        they think they're on a holiday of choice –
            past deserted homesteads they all come,

out of the woods, along the great highway,
    some stopping to admire the scene. But you
        know better – in the heart of it can see: as yet
            they're only in the suburbs of the Twilight Zone.

HERTFORD CASTLE

Winds and storms today, six people dead
because of walls, or roofs, collapsed,

a lorry on the M5 overturned,
causing carnage on its homeward journey.

I listened to the news, the weathermen
spoke of devastations yet to come –

gale-force winds to howl all night
now apocalypse has come to Hertfordshire.

But for all that we will sleep in fits and starts,
and dream of a world come to its end,

we'll wake, responsibilities intact,
to find wind dropped, to meet a fragile dawn,

and know Armageddon is postponed,
and earth not yet returned to megaliths,

but we'll need our coats and scarves tomorrow,
going out to see if Hertford Castle stands.

AS A MAN GROWS OLDER

He finds these days there are fewer faces
worth crossing the street for, fewer new books
that merit reading – he distrusts
        what critics say,

having been one himself: not painting with
a broad brush any more, he has narrowed
his sights. He feels that he is waiting
        for the last train

that never seems to come. As for the new ideas –
they're ones he's heard before, with novel names,
but if you lift the covering you'll find
        the same old cracks

visible the first time round. He rummages
the bottom-drawer, disturbs old papers, disinters
once-scrambled messages, he's looking backward
        to a future

that was never his. In doing so he knows that time
has left him little to explore. If he sees lights
they're at a distance. He is walking in his own
        new science park,

fingering the strange exhibits there. If music plays
it's from another dancing-floor than any he would choose
to dance on now – he's had his fill of the
        humanities

and their indifferent consolations.
He'd rather have a truth that's raw than any
sentimental quatsch, can no longer be content
        with language-games.

He's looking through a telescope – the view's
so different this far out from shore. It is as if
he's mending boats when boats are on an open sea –
      no starting-place

can be discerned, no firm foundations,
and not a single plank is sure: to stay afloat
you must learn what's general from particulars,
      throw overboard

fashionable luggage that has weighed you down,
the antiquated clothes you wore when you were young
and life was certain: what's merely probable suffices as
      a man grows older.

SETTING OUT FOR THE MAD ISLANDS

I have endured too long your petty virtues, convoluted crazed
    excuses – now at last I have set out from shore

onto the Sea of Sadness in my small and too-expensive boat,
    knowing what the ticket-price was worth,

and how even under clearest skies, and on a day like this, the most
    beautiful women

at the nod of an officious head withdraw from balconies. I have
    stepped out on the Bridge to Nowhere,

hidden behind security fences, truly I have grown suspicious of the
    stepping-stones

across the River of Romance. The Stream of Dreams was swallowed
    up unnoticed in the fog, and now

I look out on the Gulf of My Misgivings. As for the Wondrous
    Waterfalls, the Magnanimous Mountains –

they are off the map, though someone's staking out perimeters to
    mark the Contours of Tomorrow

as if there were still new regions to explore. This season you might
    find me in the Valley of Revulsion

or climbing the Hills of Happiness, or abseiling down the Wailing
    Walls of Yesterday,

but most likely you will find me at the Creaking Quay waiting for
    the boat that only comes

at the thirteenth hour on a day when you least expect it: we must all
    of us make haste to climb aboard

so we can then be on the voyage out across the Bay of Bile and over
the Ocean of Our Discontent

once the sexy zephyrs start to blow. Then we may land at last – a
little disgruntled it may be

but not without a sense of wonderment – at the first, but not the
best or worst, of the Mad Islands.

THE PICNICS

Some picnic that was –
sheltering under trees we watched
useless greasy papers flutter in the wind.

I admired her long brown legs revealed by shorts
(she'd always worn a dress before).
She was like a prize from the Shrovetide Fair –
this was many years ago, remember,
then girls came always with a tambourine.

Well, we didn't have the skins of seals
and when the deluge came
we set off fast across the fields.
It was no surprise the barn-roof leaked,
but that little saphead with smart sophists' words –
I still recall the slap and smack of them –
made for holes and leaks in everything.
We'd no option but to silence him.

Something else had intervened that day –
it's hard to say quite what it was –
but when skies cleared, rain ceased, the picnic over,
dismayed, we fashioned in wet straw
what seemed as much our effigies.

We took too much for granted even then.
There would be other times, of course –
those many picnics yet to come
by riversides, or lakes, or else on islands,
picnics palpable, obscure, or odd,
some where we bathed
stark naked in resplendent waters,
heard curious music, and there was no rain,
when we were fervid in the lush cool grasses

One day I shall tell you about them.

NOTES

The Velvet Band (p. 4): This borrows, though not slavishly, from a scene in a novel by the Hungarian writer Sandór Marai. In the novel (translated into German as *Wandlungen einer Ehe*) the significance of the velvet band is made *explicit* as is demanded by the laws of realistic fiction. In the poem, by contrast, I take advantage of a different medium to allow it to be *implicit*.

Nietzsche Contra Grammar (p. 8): This is Nietzsche at his most provocative. Yet, shorn of the histrionics, and of the (empty) promise of the *Übermensch*, what he returns us to is a recurring theme of philosophy since the Greeks – that we are misled by the grammar of our language, and that it is the task of the philosopher to undeceive us of the resulting fallacies.

Trouble with Workers (p. 13): The firm in question is FoxConn, operating in Taiwan, on behalf of Apple. The details of the (mis)management, scarcely a one-off either in Taiwan or China, are given in Slavoj Žižek, *The Year of Living Dangerously* (2012).

Early Days (p. 16): For most of the time that there has been life on earth that life has been bacterial. The rest of life, including daffodils, dinosaurs, and of course ourselves, is, as it were, an afterthought.

Orichalc (p. 20): Atlantis, along with the curious metal – orichalc – which distinguishes it, is the product of Plato's imagination in his old age. The (exceedingly improbable) history of the empire of Atlantis is to be found in his late works, the *Timaeus* and the unfinished *Critias*.

Remembering Leonitus (p. 22): The name of Leontius, who was clearly once a well-known Athenian citizen, occurs twice in Plato's *Republic*, both times in connection with a condition which we would nowadays think of as psychosexual. Insofar as Leontius is remembered at all it is precisely for that which – one presumes –he would most wish to be forgotten.

Pharsalus (p. 23): Here I have drawn primarily on Plutarch. It is remarkable how much time Julius Caesar spent *becoming* master of Rome and for how little time he spent in actually *ruling* it.

Dirge for the old Icelandic Poets (p. 24): Snorri Sturlusson in his *Edda* (around 1220) records the names and verse-forms of Icelandic praise-poets who served such courts as those of the kings of Norway and Earls of Orkney. The poetic forms these writers devised were so complex and demanding that any sense tended to be lost in the strangled syntax. It was a dying tradition by the time of Snorri: even the royal courts by then had had enough of them, and found their needs best served by prose-writers. The examples of verses preserved in the *Edda* do little to make one regret that most of the work of these praise-poets is lost.

The Emperor (p. 26): Rudolphine Prague is essentially the magic Prague beloved of the Surrealists, city of the golem and the alchemists. Amongst all the magic there was what we now recognize as genuine scientific achievement, for example, in Kepler's laws of planetary motion. That, however, is our perspective. It was not one available here to Rudolph's indignant courtier whose concern was to bring back what he thought of as *normality*.

London 1665 (p. 29): Defoe was only a small child at the time of the Great Plague, and in no position to be a witness of it. The narrator in *A Journal of the Plague Year*, like the protagonist of my poem, is a fictional creation.

Helmand Province (p. 41): I visited Afghanistan as a young man in 1978 when it seemed a haven of peace compared with Teheran where what we now know as the Iranian Revolution was fomenting. The Russian invasion of Afghanistan, of course, followed close on its heels.

Icelandic Saga (p. 47): I visited Iceland in 2008 at the time when the country had gone bankrupt, though it was only subsequently that I (along with most Icelanders) discovered quite what had happened. There are now many accounts of how the Icelandic bubble burst – and of how it grew in the first place. My poem only hints at some of the elements of this saga. I hope too that it gives some impression of one of the most civilized countries in the world.

John Steed (p. 58): This refers back to a now "cult" television series of the Sixties and Seventies, *The Avengers*, which might, indeed, be seen as having more style than substance. My John Steed has lost not only his Bentley but also much of his chutzpah.

Hertford Castle (p. 67): Hertford Castle, it is only fair to note, has been a ruin for many centuries.